ATTITUDE

uncollected poems of the seventies

Michael Lally

Hanging Loose Press

Hanging Loose wishes to thank the National Endowment for the Arts for a grant in support of the publication of this book.

Library of Congress Cataloging in Publication Data

Lally, Michael, 1942-
   Attitude : uncollected poems, 1970-1980.

   I. Title.
PS3562.A414A94   811'.54   82-1059
ISBN 0-914610-31-7   AACR2

Portrait of the author by Alex Katz

Layout by Zirlin Graphics
Photo by Edie Baskin

Published by Hanging Loose Press
231 Wyckoff Street
Brooklyn, NY 11217

Produced at The Print Center, Inc., Box 1050, Brooklyn, N.Y., 11202, a non-profit printing facility for literary and arts-related publications. Funded by The New York State Council on the Arts and the National Endowment for the Arts.

Some of these poems were first published in: *Blue Suede Shoes;
The Great Speckled Bird; Woodwind; The Daily Rag; Granite;
Buffalo Stamps; The Greenfield Review; Diana's BiMonthly;
Bird; december; Fag Rag; Abraxas; Clown War; Me Too; Roof;
Handbook; The World; Poetry Now; Saturday Morning; #;
The New Journal; The Washington Review; contact II; Mass
Transit; Home Planet News; Renegade; The Big House;* and
Hanging Loose.

Other books by the author: *WHAT WHITHERS* (Doones
Press 1970); *THE LINES ARE DRAWN* (Asphalt Press 1970);
MCMLXVI POEM (Nomad Press 1970); *STUPID RABBITS*
(Morgan Press 1971); *THE SOUTH ORANGE SONNETS*
(Some of Us Press 1972); *LATE SLEEPERS* (Pellet Press 1973);
MALENKOV TAKES OVER (Dry Imager 1974); *ROCKY
DIES YELLOW* (Blue Wind Press 1975); *DUES* (Stone Wall
Press 1975); *SEX/THE SWING ERA* (Lucy & Ethel 1975);
MENTALLY HE'S A SICK MAN (Salt Lick Press 1975);
MY LIFE (Wyrd Press 1975); *OOMALOOM* (Dry Imager
1975); *CHARISMA* (O Press 1976); *CATCH MY BREATH*
(Salt Lick Press 1976); *IN THE MOOD* (Titanic Books 1978);
JUST LET ME DO IT (Vehicle Editions 1978); *WHITE LIFE*
(Jordan Davies 1980); *HOLLYWOOD MAGIC* (Little Caesar
1982).

Contents: "Attitude"

AUTHOR'S NOTE

ATTITUDE is the 20th collection of my writing, bringing
together work not already included in the previous 19. The
period covered — 1970 to 1980 — has been the most prolific
since I started writing in the late 50s. A lot of the work in
those other 19 books is also from that period. ATTITUDE is
intended to complement and illuminate those other books.
The quotes that introduce each section are from my journals
for that year. I'd like to thank some of those who helped make
this work possible: Gloria Adelson, Karen Allen, Bruce Andrews,
John Ashbery, Ted Berrigan, Joe Brainard, Marty Brandel,
Suzanne Burgess, Gerald Burns, Ed Cox, Tina Darragh, Jane
DeLynn, Ray DiPalma, Tim Dlugos, Kenward Elmslie, Anne
Ferguson, Jimmy Fouratt, Ted Greenwald, Jim Haining,
Etheridge Knight, Arlene Ladden, Caitlin Lally, Lee Lally, Miles
Lally, Doug Lang, Annabel Levitt, Harry Lewis, Ellen Lukens,
George Mattingly, Bill McPherson, Kim Merker, National Endow-
ment for the Arts, New York Poets Foundation, Olga Nolla,
Ramon Osuna, P.E.N., Ana Ross, Donna Schlegel, Sylvia
Schuster, Robert Slater, Janey Tannenbaum, Terence Winch,
and Rain Worthington, as well as the editors and publishers of
this collection: Bob Hershon, Dick Lourie, and Ron Schreiber.

1970

"Today is more of the same. In the closed circle I have fashioned. In the alien language of another tribe. I make these documents for some heart who will recognize me truthfully. Who will know what I am and what I wanted beneath the maze of meanings and attitudes that shape the reality of everything. Beneath the necessity of talking or the necessity for being angry or beneath the actual core of life we make reference to digging deep into some young woman, and listening to her come."

-LeRoi Jones *Words*

I WAS BORN WITH A STOMACH ACHE

I was born with a stomach ache. not being able to see very
well, it being dark, shades drawn, sky cloudy, i thought about
how i would die. at first it was cancer, then later that changed.
but it was always in the stomach between the ages of 42 and
46. it made me unafraid of death and the opinions of others,
in the long run, but in the short it made me a glutton for
praise and human respect and a coward for fear i would never
leave my mark on the world i thought i had inherited, not
invented.

i ran into things. cried at old people in the streets for living
longer than i would, imagined i was love, and refused to
surrender to anyone else's dreams. in 1945 i ended the war,
celebrated my 3rd birthday and brought thousands of my
brothers and hundreds of my sisters home to resume respon-
sibilities i had carried alone through the dark. in the end they
put mirrors in all my houses and called themselves "going
blind" in order to become arbiters of my will. two years later
i told them all i was a genius and to look out. they decided
i would become famous and make over 200,000 dollars and
share it with them. for this reason they never mentioned my
stomach ache, which was growing worse.

in the year 1950 i turned 8, fell in love, inherited
anti-communism and believed in a god who loved me. the
stomach ache was her unwillingness to love me in return
without a lot of silliness and adult imitations. o goddamn i
hated that pain in the center of my body that described hell
as the absence of a beauty only my secret knowledge could
understand. i rolled in my bed and remembered naked child-
hood games behind bushes that had seemed as dense as
the jungle but through which any adult could see us as they
rode by on the highway in their henry j's and kaiser frazers.
i played with myself and remembered how foolish it had all
seemed so long ago when i was 5 and thought there was only
one great confession at 7 when i must be sorry for all the

11

games of doctor and tickle and caught you in the bathroom with your pants down and tell the priest what an evil child i had been and for ever after refrain from any such sin, from all sin in fact, until i died between 42 and 46 and god took me to his bosom as i now wished she would. but now i knew that confession was endless, that therefore so was sin, and under the covers, with my sisters asleep across the room, i thought of something i didnt know anything about with my hands between my legs and cried, the pain in my stomach, the absence of her.

now when i touch the children as i walk in the streets they all sing "wallflower, wallflower," and it reminds me of the little drummer boy who changed sex to communion and war to a pair of closed eyelids out of which stare the nephews and nieces of those second world war brothers and sisters. o, how many collars and necks will be worn thin before i knew it wasnt cancer but a bullet from a 45 service revolver? because as the necks wear, if they're white, they get red, but as the collars, if they're blue: white. i must have been 11 or 12, she had a slight mustache and worked somewhere to remind me of a ladies room attendant, but maybe that was only a case of sitting on a hard metal folding chair outside the door and keeping teenagers away with a fly swatter and flashlight. i dont know. but under the boardwalk she played with me not like i was a porcelain doll or a genius but as though i were already dying from the bullet hole in my gut. and i felt it. the pain expanded. her mustache grew moist. tom & jerry, a 15 year old italian from jersey city and a 17 year old jew from brooklyn, with their respective smooth lipped girl friends, made love under the stars like trying to jump over gas station signs advertising penn oil. under the boardwalk i pushed back with my own dream of being rocked to sleep in my big mama's lap, and later it would seem almost as lonely for her.

in 1956 we all bought white tee shirts, black chinos, white sweat socks and black pointy toed slip ons with tassels. we rolled up the sleeves of the tee shirts in neat half inch layers. we stuck stogies in between our yellow teeth. we gathered on the boardwalk between the pinball machines and the juke box with "egghead" and "annie had a baby, cant work no more" on it and we took off in rows of threes to march on the bungalow of a new york jewish intellectual of 15 who had stolen an angel's kisses. we had lain in bed all summer dreaming of her between our thighs. we had seen her in the mirror when we let go of ourselves. and we had believed she had to go to the toughest men in town, along with the free games on the pinball machines, the nickel on a string that made the juke box go for free, and the pistol that the puerto rican dropped when the cop shot him down across the street from the boardwalk, across the street from jerry lee lewis shakin on, across the street from the lady and old man who kept their hands buried in the change pockets of their aprons while we watched our angel's so beautifully curved belly that was the sign of a nonvirgin as we all had been told by those who knew. just look for the curve of the belly swelling ever so slightly and then back again to follow the contours of the ass and you know you have a woman with experience on your hands. but the same thing on a man means a kid who pulls his pod too much. we all stared hard at our bellies in the mirror after the bath, i thought i could see the pain make it swell and wondered if at last god hadnt rewarded me for my sins. but at least my lips were thin, for everyone knew that on a white man fat lips meant blow job, cocksucker, fag. and when we tried to buy rubbers from the kid who sold snow cones at kiddy land he said he had to see our things first to measure the size so he could make sure we didnt get rubbers that would be too small, or would fall off when our angel finally told us to meet her under the boards, and after the kiddies went home, on the merry-go-round under the tarpaulin darkness the fat-lipped snow cone boy measured the thing of a boy who had already spent a year in reform school for stealing all his mothers money and running away, a boy who had been beaten in a wrestling match by an intellectual 15 year old jew from long island despite the fact that the jew

13

was a jew and the boy was a muscle bound hybrid of irish
and german, and when he told me about it i made him feel
so bad he cried and promised me he'd never do it again. i
never got the rubbers that year because i told the fat lipped
snow cone boy he would be castrated if he came near me or
my buddy again. o god and the stomach of my 14th year was
in my head as we marched down that dark summer street in
our glowing white tee shirts, the sparks from our stogies
lighting the way. the muscle bound buddy was gone again
and i was alone with an angel so dark i couldnt see her,
crawling like the baby boy we had last year, into the room
where we keep my stomach ache now. but the police came
before one shot was fired and the jew went home to long
island, the angel to an off duty gi who could do the dirty
boogie. i got arrested a week later for stabbing a guy with an
ice pick.

GREASE BLUES

when i grow up i wanna be
a rocknroll drummer named jimmy death
& play all the festivals
with my hair greased back to the floor
and both feet workin like the pistons
in your heart when theres a knock on the door
& dope on the floor & you aint expectin nobody

when i grow up i wanna be
a rocknroll drummer named jimmy death
& snow all the women
with my hair greased back below my ass
and my third leg talkin for my third eye
& my pockets overflowin with the good stuff
& my face a free pass to everybodys jam

when i grow up i wanna be
a rocknroll drummer named jimmy death
& deal with the people
who treated me like food
when my hair was combed back over my leather
& the poetry in my hog sent shivers down the spines
of the people who would sell the weather
& getting it together meant an hour ago

when i grow up i wanna be
a rocknroll drummer named jimmy death
& pay back the pigs who kept the sun out
& get it back for you & me

MAY 4, 1970

tonite the kent students died
what am i supposed to do
last year it was james rector
what were you supposed to do
a couple of years before that
it was Orangeburg what were we
supposed to do four white students
to pile on top of the heap of blacks
two women and two men young bodies
to pile on top of the black bodies
on top of the red bodies & what
were you supposed to do about
the four kent students and
the orangeburg students and the
james rectors and sammy younges
and the four little girls in
that church and the nameless
dead and you all alone

THE OTHER NIGHT

I went out on the balcony
to watch the helicopters
circle over the campus
about a mile away.

My neighbor came out
on his balcony, just back
from Nam and up for a few
medals. We figured the
number of choppers: 4.
We figured the number of
National Guardsmen. He had
heard 800 out at the base;
I'd heard about a thousand
on underground FM.

Our wives were inside with
the kids. His watching tv
waiting for the ice to get hard.
Mine making something, anything,
to not be not making something,
anything, going over in her mind
the arguments she had for insisting
I get a gun.

My neighbor in his GI haircut
and tattoos and straight legged
pants (me in my hair and bells
and tattoo and straight legged past
— he collects guns, I argue —)
motions toward the campus. I
follow his gesture and see clouds
coming from the choppers. My
neighbor calculates the wind and
estimates the time it'll take
to reach us.

THAT FEELING
6.1 70 (remembering 7.4.62 AWOL)

if i write a poem this time for you
it isn because i love you, love is
a superstar on amateur night and we
arent amateurs anymore, any of us.
And it isnt because i owe you anything,
I owe it all to myself, like everyone.
But maybe it's because of that feeling
when you see the rocky mountains the
first time after driving all night
through kansas, or figure out why we
have come to where we are and so can
guess where we might be heading. . .
you know, it's the feeling you get
when you find out who you are . . . i mean
you want to tell someone, you want to
stretch out your hand and tap another
human being on the shoulder and say
hey, see them clouds, theyre not clouds,
theyre the snow capped rocky mountains,
and we just rode all night through kansas
and even if it is the fourth of july
we're gonna go right up to the top and
have a few joints and a snowball fight.

ANOTHER CONVENIENT MYTH

well, talking to people around the country who have been
in the movement in one way or another, the feeling everybody
seems to have is, i want out. or, i want a piece of the peace
& quiet of straight life for awhile. or the long hair version
of straight life which is slowly becoming the straight life of
our time. another casualty. another buffalo bill and digger
dan. a brilliant mind lost to the mediocrity of delivering
groceries for another five years until it's too late to move
because your stomach gets in the way, or your wife and kids or
your husband and kids or your lack of either. what they seem
to be saying is: i thought it would take care of itself. but
it didnt. for the rest of us, well, isnt it easier to blame
the ones who stick it out if anything goes wrong than to blame
those who started the whole thing? only they have forgotten
so soon that it wasnt us who started it, it was them. only,
now they arent sure there is a them. another convenient myth.

1971

"You can't change everything even if everything is changed."

-Gertrude Stein *Ida*

SHORT STORY

Not interested, he said, and backed out the door, one hand on the door knob the other on his gun. Blam. That was the door, said the man to his wife who had turned around expecting to see her husband shot through the head. But her husband wasnt shot through the head he was standing perfectly still in the middle of the room sweating. It was August in Washington DC, a very humid town. She grabbed the old 357 magnum down from the mantel piece and ran to the screen door which had only seconds before slammed shut behind the masked man. Not interested? she said beneath her dress, hmmmph, and she opened the door and fired. She killed the mailman.

SHORTER STORY

By the time he got back there were two of them . . .
one for you and one for me, he thought, hanging up his
hand on the hand rack. This is the beginning of everything
said the woman and sat on his head as he settled into a
relaxed position on the couch. Well, he thought, without
saying anything, being in a compromising position, well,
he thought, there's nothing to say. This wasnt the only
time it worked that way. Everyday it gets a little closer.
By the time she stood up there were four more.

WAITING

These young and these
young, as though 1956
or 1873 or the T'ang Dynasty

Don't they realize it is 1970
and everything has already happened

we all want to go back
to the old rock n roll
dip dip bam dip dip bam

MAKE BELIEVE BALLROOM TIME

in the doorways of open apartments and musty storerooms
on the side of a hill and under the ruins of some gas station
these good times we write our poems out of
become, becoming, are and were, the air
that moves through all those things
and even in the abandoned refrigerators on the old porches
the rusty sleds in the cellar

we *can* find some atmosphere that gives
as well as takes away

SORRY

always for the air, the atmosphere
of my personal ark, in which my two
children have grown from my sides
and you have found me barefoot and
open head, the hair falling away waves,
the imagination elicits fond remarks
from the roaches and bats of my ark's
apartments. And my children as yet
speak no language in common. I hear
them shouting beneath the deck, can
only judge from their tone that they
are angry with the side that made them.
The one from the left wishes to have
been born of the right, that of the
right from the left.

                 And the hallways
creak with the night air, with the
distant stars, with the salty bats.
And the atmosphere of my personal ark
becomes denser and denser emitting
the cool acid of what our foreheads
have in common. The wrinkles not of
age, but of a national condition. I
almost forgot,

               I'm sorry too for all
I have left behind me, stranded in the
flood of a perception that cannot
recognize the isolated individual in
all this. If it is not in pairs, if
it does not acknowledge the walls of
our hallways, if it refuses to accept
our defintion of breathing as a salute,
then it must be left behind in the mud
never to witness our new world of the
personal ark of everyones atmosphere.

Those without arks become history's victims
those others, you and you, we sail on
and on and on.
                    Life is life.

REVOLUTION

okay, touching and then
opening the wounds for
the salt you always carry
for just such occasions

this hotel is 29 stories
high and we been up and
we been down, and we been
up and down but this time
it's the hotel or us

cant do it, cant seem to
do it the way we were
used to it, maybe because
there used to be so few
of us to start doing it
and we were always up for
the sounds of our own

this many times i've been
awake all night and we
still continue to act as
though we were sleeping

one of these days it's
gonna mean getting up and
walking, only this time
without the artificial moon.

JAMMIN
for S.

sniffin scags a death bag sister
i said momma it's the mans trick
the fat man who owns the carnival
cuts the cards loads the dice is
made of smack and runs speed in
his veins to feed his empty sleeves
got fake pockets in his brain
he fills them up with you, momma
he aint death but he knows its sister
and covers its wife's debts

layin back on a brand new bed
of roses that begin to bleed, it
aint your roses sister, it's your
head, a bed of iodine and melted
plastic used for the manufacture
of war games: he wins you lose,
he wins you die, he wins you pay,
he wins you grow like a candle:
down to the ground til you dis
appear, he wins, sister, scag is
a death bag, a trick dick, a
lovely, muffled, slow motion
kick to the ass of your brain.
kick back, kick back, kick back.

BIG BUSINESS

enough isnt enough

HONKY HILL (HYATTSVILLE MARYLAND)

no blacks
upstairs orientals
and out back
downstairs rednecks
some indians
many latin, mexican,
puerto rican

in the air shaft:
ya got nice hair
why would I lie
for christs sake
you're 12 years old
you wanna spend
the rest of your life
with straw on your
head like me? and
bleaching and fixing
it all the time just
to look decent, o
why cantchu leave it
the way you were born

beam ceilings look good
but all it means is:
no insulation, so noise
level is 850% above
that necessary to drive
white mice to biting
each others eyes out

two abandoned cars
in the parking lot
both red, both convertible
both with 4 flats
both swarmed on by kids
both related somehow to
the men who never come out

MY SON

blond, unlike us
blue eyed, unlike
us, white skinned

john coltrane: my
son has never and
will never be one

he has never lived
when men had not walked
on the moon, or col
trane was alive or
i was a young man

he refuses to learn
keeps falling from
high places on his head
his blond, white,
blue-eyed head, no,
he doesnt refuse to
learn, he just keeps
falling

OUT IN THE HALL

out in the hall
the sweeper, he
comes here every morning
about this time
and whistles to
all of us hiding behind our doors

would he be a famous composer if
or a wealthy song writer from nashville
should he have stepped on people
left his wife & kids at his mothers place
decided never to sweep anyone elses dirt
made it on his guts and determination
what was he going to be when
he found himself with a broom and
the halls outside all our doors

through the open
window we can
hear the echo of
his whistle as he
carries his broom
to the next place
it sounds a little like
the kind of tune you wake up
in the morning humming but
cant remember where you heard it
what its name is or why it makes you
feel so young, so early summer morning
the old lady upstairs says.
god bless, god bless the sweeper man

BEGINNING WITH BUSES

the things we can miss
about the city, sister

not just riding in a bus
but flash on the kids
hanging on the back, up
on the rear bumper, for
a free ride uptown

                    even
now sometimes when the
sun comes up in a clear
sky and the animals all
lay down their heads to
sleep together like a
good family, even now,
there are things we miss

the excitement of discovering
some hole-in-the-wall dive
that has a juke box with at
least one number on it no
one has heard for decades,
or no one has ever heard

and what did we call those days
when it rained and we all stayed
in our apartments only sticking
our faces and tongues out the
windows from time to time —
no place out here in the country
could ever be as quiet, as alone,
as complete as your own room on
one of those gray rainy days in
the city

           big business on the street/
street rags/subways/unexpected parks/
basketball games/flea markets/street
musicians/tough kids/coffee houses
that didnt care how long you sat
around or how much you spent/the
people
           there must be a way to save that
too

ERIC DOLPHY

eric dolphy blew my brains out
eric dolphy blew his heart out
eric dolphy blew away big business under berlin
eric dolphy in international waters
eric dolphy at midnight on east tenth in spring of 1961
eric dolphy looking through me
eric dolphy signing away the air
eric dolphy jack hammer
eric dolphy in the tree
eric dolphy between you and me
eric dolphy under duress
eric dolphy in the army, airforce, marines, navy, coast guard
eric dolphy in love
eric dolphy walking without shoes
eric dolphy against the wall
eric dolphy pushing organs around
eric dolphy watching old shirley temple movies with bo robinson
eric dolphy sitting down to lunch
eric dolphy walking away
eric dolphy riding in a taxi uptown
eric dolphy hungry, eating milky ways, smelling fresh cooked
            chicken upstairs
eric dolphy watching me move
eric dolphy following me home
eric dolphy dying on my wedding day
eric dolphy dying on your wedding day
eric dolphy dying
eric dolphy dead
eric dolphy silent
eric dolphy laying down
eric dolphy falling down
eric dolphy not moving
eric dolphy gone
eric dolphy back again

HIDE, GO AHEAD

behind your cock
behind your shoulder length
behind your beard and balls
behind your eye brows and furry insides
behind your black eye shadow, lip shadow, ear shadow, throat
        shadow
behind your lips, your lines
behind your private business
behind your too long from home away
behind your lanced meat on the picket fence of your half smile
        half frown down
behind your backyard mind
behind your funky coal dealer shoeless idea of a horse and buggy
        defense
behind your sold out tickets to the revolutionary ball
behind your sand gazing .
behind your whistling the theme song from the movie you hope
        to star in
behind your never whistling, never walking backwards, never
        waving goodby
behind your sweet sticky fingers licked
behind your blues rendition of something gay
behind your hearing aid shaped like the latest rolling stone
behind your dress up day where you ride out to meet the foe in
        full armor
behind your dreams of being loved
behind your dreams of loving
behind your fantasy of what it is like to be you
behind your behind full of stable ideas
behind your beautiful but neglected behind
behind your blessed imitation of one of us
behind your grace, your amazing way with people who never
        knew you before
behind your need to be missed, be ignored, be forgotten
behind your you me his their her my your you self
behind

40

WHY NOT TAKE ALL OF IT

for all of us I mean
theres something beautiful
about so many things and
because my skin turns red
in the hot sun means I aint
supposed to touch her black
brown yellow thighs or sleep
in his dreams of a little bit
Mao a little bit Tao a little
bit Nkrumah a little bit Black
Elk a little bit John Sinclair
or the hair of a curly head a
greasy straight haired fried
head of kinks and blonde locks
whats wrong with the Grand
Canyon and Times Square both
or Albert Ayler behind Elvis
shit, you got a name for every
thing blame the european for
inventing labels and then call
him a peckerwood redneck cracker
snatching fool of a pink pig skinned
sexless un man talking about men as
though women werent good for anything
but them, why not whats good for all
for all? the little good in everything
for everybody and the bad to the dogs
who dig it, dig it? you know, I remember
you talking bad acting to the woman I loved
in 1960 because she wouldnt have any of your
stuff and she was black and beautiful and so
were you you said putting down this paddy cats
greyness while you went home to a grey woman of
your own, and you did say "own" brother, another
Western White Eyes conception forgetting the earth

and all things on it are ours to share and fuck the
man who thinks it's all there for him to ball or eat or
lay on alone, mother earth, some of us white boys and our
white sisters are coming home, with or without brother ted joans

in 1962 I was living in an Air
Force barracks in Rantoul Illi
nois/had a dark inverted V on
the upper sleeves of my uniform
where my Airman Third Class stri
pes had been before I went AWOL
to San Francisco and got courts
martialled/over my locker I had
a picture of an old friend from
Jersey who I often called when
drunk so we could moan and groan
to each other across 1500 miles
she was attractive to me and a
down, good people but to our mu
tual friends she was homely with
her flat black face and skinny
round shoulders/a new guy came
in one afternoon when I was on
guard duty and I showed him his
bunk/he walked up and down the
aisle between the bunks looking
at the one picture allowed over
everyones clothes locker/he came
back to the desk and sitting on
it with his big muscled country
boy ass and fullback thighs said
I see we got a nigger in here &
a ugly nigger at that/I asked
what made him say that and he got
up and walked to my bunk and then
pointed to the picture of my old
friend and lover Delores/it was
her high school picture in one of
those grey paper frames with the
ragged white edge/she had invited
me to her prom in East Orange &

I had declined because I couldnt
get leave but I went AWOL anyway
and she had her date take her to
New York City and drop her off
where she met me in Washington
Square and then went to bed on the
couch at a friends apartment/I
wasnt caught that time/this time
I walked up to the big country boy
and said "Thats my wife." as quietly
as I could to still be heard/he
turned red faced and started to say
something about nigger-/I pulled
my nail clippers combination file
from my pocket and told him if he
ever said anything to me again or
I heard he had said something about
me or my wife I would guarantee I
would take at least one of his eyes
out before he killed me which I was
sure he could do with his meaty red
hands/I held the nail file open &
glared at him/another guy watched
from the doorway to the latrine/I
guess I meant it/sometimes I told
guys I'd puncture their ear drums
with a pencil if they fucked with
me/this big bear sort of grunted
& actually looked frightened/he
finally walked away and never
bothered me again, like most of
the guys who in that barracks
happened to be all white/I never
told Delores/I did ask her to
marry me one time/we had an ar
gument about babies/when/how
many/it was an excuse to call it

off/I went away/I hear she is on
the nod quite often in Washington
Square/I now have two blonde babies

OUR GANG

shit. this dude
1960-1 our time,
the editors daughter . . . my main man
nodding all afternoon instead of . . .
getting them together because I love
that motherfucker, have always had

the editors daughter to europe to "forget"
comes back knocked up, nervous, still good people
gets two kids, tough times, chelsea life until
she splits for bolinas in the mid-sixties

I write stories, poems, plays,
musicals, songs, sermons, all
about contrast, white/black and
the final solution: pollution
do it up, mix it up, blue eyed
freckle faced spades . . . shit.

can you relate to our gang forming
in the late fifties making it a hot damn trip of 60-61
dispersing into the psychedelic sixties of midwestern
teenyboppers fantasies . . . san francisco was a bitch bro
but newark and E.O. in 1-9-6-0 put a spell on me . . .

BEEN

blind for 29 years now
splayed wound flack trap blandness
phony for 29 years now
shushed fracture uniform Magi
flush for 29 years now
Aryan dispossessed oval bookish
foul for 29 years now
dipped flamboyant reverb shank
rake for 29 years now
loons whined descent blaster rip
docile for 29 years now
jam architecture freeze shudder
grey for 29 years now
step jimson flight carrion shaker
dangerous for 29 years now
visionary pyramid omega rapacious
solid for 29 years now
landscape conspire frame shopped
dumb for 29 years now

FUCK FANTASIES

thats all over
meeting you like this
in a conspiracy of pride

dig blackamerica with a
beauty pageant just like
national anthem just like
flag & songs about MAN just like
maybe not just (smile) but *like*

no one ever stood up on america
& sang the way we want to be but
cant walk away from to remember

community baby, we got a
case out on you, we do,
& when it comes up, it comes
in time for the new people

maybe they wont have to walk away

SO THEY HELPED EACH OTHER OUT . . .

On the balcony Joe Hill
does his funny imitation of
Joan Baez, we're all laughing
and shouting getting pie eyed
on rum. Nobody seems to mind
that there is no hash, no, oh
the hills of Bolinas remin'us
of

    In the 1970s it was
left alone to see for itself.
We kept to our beds, afraid.
Some Latin Americans, poets,
stuffed themselves on Indians
and miners and peasant women
with beaded smiles that only
shone on clearest December days.
When they got off the boat
we werent there to wave or throw eagles.

1972

"She ended by choosing a dress with a hole in its sleeve. The last time she had worn it, she had stood before a restaurant which was too luxurious, too ostentatious, which she was frightened to enter, but instead of saying: 'I am afraid to enter here,' she had been able to say: 'I can't enter here with a hole in my sleeve.' "

-Anais Nin
A Spy in the House of Love

<u>3/21/72</u>

the only ones who arent afraid to look like fools
are the fools —
                    !

                ah, I wish I was music

(1962 bringing heroin in three small packets in my
tennis shoes back from new york to chicago to the
base down by rantool having gone AWOL again to see
my friends my women my city myself carrying this as
a favor drunk and dangerous to discover when Scotty
snorts it that Ralphy sold me some soap powder for
fifteen dollars cheap)

        "wanting what we need keeps us
          from getting what we want   "

                        —Elliott Coleman

        *   *

"well, I dont know" John, 1972, G'town,
"scag can be pretty nice" or "I mean,
scag is a pretty nice drug" then "I
dont like the idea of something" or "not
being able" then *"depending* on anything"

            *

Mao says put down your enemy in strategy
but respect him/her in *tactics*

                                            53

3/25/72 CHILDREN'S MARCH

Jesse Jackson has the crowd chant
"we are black" "WE ARE BLACK" "we are brown"
"WE ARE BROWN"

"we are beautiful"

"WE ARE BEAUTIFUL"
"and we are proud"

"WE ARE PROUD!"

and there's Caitlin and Miles — *pink!* — rosy
cheeked from the bitter wind — beautiful

— too

CAITLIN
(age 4)

1: fragile as imagination's
   rays of expectation

   I love you so much
   I'm afraid I'll never let you go . . .

2: we have met and decided your future

   to keep us from you, from her, and each other

   wondering if it is true you will be you

3: when I touch you

   bernadine dorn comes out of hiding
   at the head of an army of amazons

   when you touch me
   i am no longer alone

4: I'll try all the best ways I know how to
   not depend on you
   forever

FRANK O'HARA

i despised an effete new york elitist fag in lunch poems 64
but stayed with them because . . .

until i began to touch inside myself the places where the wit
& polished camp gave way to poignancy & the true romantic/city
kind/20th century shallow but intense kind/until that gave way
to the human soft & afraid & i saw frank o'hara lining my dreams
with this: the way to be yourself & survive . . . but he didnt &
was he?

to break away & be real, yeah we all shrug and say: what the fuck
does that mean/ but we all continue to look for ourselves in others
anyway

T.B. SHEETS

this is the way berrigan says it: "big-a-mist"
like the italian fog joke
he is still proud of his electricians union card
i still say "i come from a family of cops"

THE WORLD IS SO INTERESTING IF YOU JUST LET IT

his eye

        clocked

    she sucks   (this is the
                              this is the
                              this:

                                  etc.

dark, sulphurous, young, spring wound woman
black lace sheer dress through which everything
everyone & she wasted stumbling this & this

fair,
      graphic, young, air cooled man
cream satin tight dress from which much plus
everyone & he anticipation jerk & this this

"Oooo!" she to him "you cunt" touching
"ooooO!" he to her "you ⸺" grabbing

I would like you to be my husband & wife

her eye
        his thigh

             fingers

    tongue fucked nostrils

                      this is this

THIS

my breath cha-chas in my throat

the 50s tremble in my limbs & tongue

my heart fills with footsteps, fighting dogs

I am afraid to fight or face this man alone

SEASONS GREETINGS

The pillow is flat & the mattress exchanges bones with the floor
Xmas is coming again soon
Alley reminders of holidays past & the bums in them
Television static has the kids all screaming and scratching the glass
Open the refrigerator, a woman's voice saying
For dinner we all sit around and smell the money like dogs

"DYLAN'S VOICE CRACKS"

he's gettin old

I was a baby when he was a baby

in New York we demanded to be accepted

I was afraid to be taken for a tourist

I wanted to live in one of them houses
on MacDougal he lives in now

I lost the contest when I was 15 singing
O Donna O Donna and only my date clapped

my voice cracked

Dylan's gettin old

TRYING NOT TO SCRATCH

I used to be detached
in the "service"
you take baby cream
spread it on your sky blue suede hip huggers
walk to the drugstore fast
pick up the rear bumper on a 1970 Toyota Corolla
slip in the city dog shit
spend a quiet evening at the only bar within walking distance

"scabbies" somehow makes me think of the navy
I have never been on a ship or "in the navy"
I have been in the Air Force and
I have been depressed over a bad case of "scabbies"
in fact that's why I'm writing this down
it also makes me think of taxi cabs in downtown Manhattan
which makes me think of you
all of you

our Catholic youth punishes us into thinking of Allen Ginsberg
as sad when in fact he is only lonely like everyone else
sometimes, in fact Monday evening, May 8th, 1972 at 8:30 P.M.
at the New York 92nd Street YMHA Poetry Center, I am sad
this time because they are taking my picture
over and over again and I have just washed my hair
in some stranger's apartment with his shampoo
which makes the hair stick together in stringy strands
and look dull and thin and skinny and
they are offering me all kinds of free liquor
but I never drink so all I have is ice water
and they ask me to sign my name in the book
and my name appears under the pen I'm holding
while above it I read the signature: Anais Nin
and afterwards it's raining and my old Jersey buddies
and my old girlfriend and her ex-husband — the only
white person besides me — go across the street to meet
a bunch of other white friends, including 2 "revolutionary faggots"

from Washington DC and one stranger from New York
in fact with the shampoo that ruined my debut and
a young poetry entrepeneur who keeps reminding me
of Ted Berrigan and Simon Schuchat and I hate to remind people
of other people, later Jim Bertolino shows up with his wife Lois
but too late to see Harvey Shapiro who introduced me without
knowing me but who knew me well enough to introduce me in a way
that made me understand how obvious I am to everyone but myself
and said he wanted to have one drink with me because
he really liked my stuff and I could tell he meant it
but I dont drink

1973

"Human consciousness moves, but it is not
a leap; it is one inch. One inch is a
small jump, but that jump is everything.
You go way out and then you have to come
back — to see if you can move that inch."

-Philip Guston *Big Sky 5*

AMAZING CELLS HEAL
for Barbara Boogie

I love to dance &
                love everyone then
lose "it all" in the movement the action of air & grace &
                        soft spots following hard
I love to dance
                get so goddamned carried away in the flow
                my finger bleeds, splits from joint to tip
                along the seams & curls that identify me
                somewhere in this city
my finger tip splits & splits as I snap it &
throw a hip at anyone who wants it
I love to dance
                the air at a party if it's too dark & not too
                dry or smoky & not *too* dark
that air divides
                the way we want to when we can't make up
                our minds or are afraid to
it lets us in and just the way we are, no complaints or
                movement analysis
                                we move, that's all
& move the air that others move to & that is where we join
it is as subtle as the touch we waited for
that first time we trembled to be touched
it's all in the air
                we pour into the energy of all those
                years waiting to be touched instead of
                touching
I love to dance
                & am amazed when days later reading a poem
                I absently rub my longest finger with my
                thumb & realize the flesh has healed again
                & it's Thursday & there's a party or dance
                this Saturday night & I have been alone
                in bed all week waiting to be touched so

Saturday night I'll touch myself again to
air & other waves we make & the skin of
my finger will break again from snapping
so hard & I wont know it till the next
morning when I'll wake alone & show it to
whoevers around & say

       I sure do love to
         dance

it might begin anywhere

                              finger tip
                               tongue

     tip between knuckles

                                      nipple so far away
                                    neck   back
                                      hairline

cracks
everywhere
knee pit
arm back
hip fold
thigh bend
double cheeks with wing

                             salt sings in them
                         flesh floods
                                     the atmosphere
                                   tongue tip
                                   nostrils
                                   what
                                   wings

higher
tit hair
eye lash
down each vertebra sucked
                         flesh pocket

                                cell orgasm
                                skin orgasm
                                toe suck
                                ear fuck
                                tongue fuck

                                                  oral
                                                  anal
                                                  smile
cheek to clit
back to tit
cock to pit of neck and soft shoulder
ball to thigh to cock to mouth to asshole to tongue to cunt to
                                        quick bites everywhere
person to person to
                  cock to cock to
                            pussy to prick to
                                        cheeks to cheeks to
instructions for the dance
                            begin anywhere
                                        eye to eye . . . say

70

business is bad
theres this guy
wants to be hanged
only he owns the rope
thinks tying the knot is magic
and he's the magician only
he wants to be entertained
doesnt like our magic
the way we make it
wants us to do it his way only
each way is different
so we do it our way
he has us figured
tells us where to go
tells us we will meet him there
only we go to meet ourselves there
and he isnt us
maybe we arent either till we get there
and maybe we'll never get there
but we go anyway
and he sees us going
and he wants us to go with him
and then he wants us to hang him
but he owns the rope
and his knot is magic
and wants us all to know him
like he thinks he knows us
so that if he ever really does
convince somebody they want to hang him
we'll all feel like theyre hanging
a piece of ourselves
and then he'll really have the power
not just once a week
but maybe for generations and generations
maybe for two thousand years
if we fall for that shit again

I AM MY OWN CRAZY SAINT TOUCH ME HERE

the forces collecting for some giant struggle, coming up soon,

relatively,

the women, some of, coming out of sleep to lead the "warm" forces

against

the "cold" led by men who never sleep, mostly.

too

turn it around:

write it

down but not out. yes. come from where to be here not there.

yes. say:

this is how it is felt through these vectors of the cosmic forces called:

I AM MY OWN CRAZY SAINT TOUCH ME HERE.

"The disciples of light have never invented anything but
not very heavy darkness."
-Robert Desnos

driving lifetime terrycloth legs
she mounts gravity's dome: bright yellow
carbon throb of image ache
                        bump bump: BLISS!!!

The life you live may be very heavy darkness
or variants of very heavy darkness
if you concentrate on this you learn to see
the light between the shadows that make up darkness
this is where the energy forms
that helps the people in these places to live better
which is why we are always doing better
even when we are doing worse

have you ever noticed this phenomenon known as: TRUE BLISS!

cocaine & fucking
thats what she said
me in her dreams
with them & "it"
wondering what to do
call that frustration
wondering who to do it with
call that exploitation
wondering if it's worth it
call that desperation
spending your dreams
wondering about others
call that sensitivity
others are busy doing
what they are doing
cocaine & fucking

DOING
for Will

I should have said *you*
the sparks & stars "alight"
overlapping fringes:
        1) "place"
        2) partition
        3) creation
        4) place

I should have written
"what" we are always becoming
"we are always becoming" alike
"what" the variant & energy source
for "becoming" & "always" etc.

I should have held out my arms
"what" was/is in them / can be
& you & you & you & not "you"!

I should have wrestled my voice
holding on to the level that unfolds
into "what" each of us can *feel*
"Do we have to *hear* it?!"
"Do we etc."
Of course not

there are some contradictions
that no amount of "struggle"
can reconcile & these we call:
"what we are always becoming"

You should have gone on without me
You did
This is the question: "Did I?"

no "way" friend
this is what the trees teach me
like them I learn slow
& each tree quietly is "what"
it is becoming
always

I should have been precise, love
instead of just the weakness in
my language that is not becoming
weak I should have listened for
you
     but then, I did what I should
have
     this is to say I cant go back

KIDS

the kids are usually crying
the kids are usually complaining
the kids are often whining
the kids are mostly inconsiderate
the kids are a pain in the ass
the kids can be angelic & offer the most
rewarding relationships this person has ever known
the kids are contradictions like the rest of us
but the kids are always with us
while the rest of us sometimes
disappear

SHE COMES OUT OF THE DARK

she leans over me and I can smell
yes it's some sort of artificial
odor only what is "artificial" if
you can smell it! me who hates
the thought of deodorant, which
I've never used in fact, my Irish
Catholic aversion to phony smells,
I am removed from any sense of time
or place by this strange and
overwhelmingly subtle aroma that
comes from her, then I smell *her*
& it's even better, like two acts
in a great play or forgetting who
you were waiting to hear when the
warm-up act at a concert is so
terrific you let it all out right
away like some music ignorant teeny
bopper and now she settles down
beside me and I cant explain how
beautiful I know I am to be here

we dont wait because we've waited
so long, maybe seven years if you
count the first time I cheated
from her in geology class and knew
this was a person who had a sense
of herself like I only thought us
Eastern big city ethnics did because
our parents told us so many times
to be proud of ourselves that we
understood there was something they
werent proud of about us and that
made us angry and gave us style!

us *white* kids! Too! it didnt matter
like everything else I ever thought
did, only when stars finally go out
teaching us that we *can* learn
and from anything! anybody!
so we learn all night long and
in the morning it reminds us of
how it used to be possible to
"cheat" because it was possible
not to cheat but now it's all
cheating! that's us! first we
were thugs, afraid to be frightened
then beatniks and hipsters afraid
to be fools, a way to be "American"
without being what they were or
what we had been, and one day we
were hippies living on love and not
afraid to be anything but old
until they made us old we thought,
and decided to kill them for it
not being afraid of hate either
so we were weathermen and listened
to our hearts beat fast as we
trashed the cities that made us
romantics until we could let our
hair down and cry and be the
weak soft frightened male kids
we started out afraid to be but
tonight, this morning, last
night, we can be what we were always
becoming, or maybe just became like
that, snap, overnight: the cheaters!
that's all we do mom & dad is cheat
because the rules that divided us
from them and you from me and me from
me from me from me are just a form of
conceptual art now, we admire it

when we're in the mood, when we're not
we ignore it or carry it out or play
some other game that doesnt mean more
than the realization that we can be
what we always wanted to be or the
part of that that doesnt cost too much

SOMETHING REALLY STRANGE

I thought it was necessary to
cultivate a style & voice to
be recognized by those who do

I never did it anyway I just
thought it was necessary and
decided I wouldnt be one of
those recognized by one of
those who cultivate a style
& voice to be recognized by
others who also do the same

FOR THE BEAUTIFUL PEOPLE

Let us respect this
Artificial nudity
As though it were
Our mother's dress.

Knees and long legs,
Flesh like legs,
Flesh like hair,
Flesh like eyes,
Arms, and fine fingers.

I respect your
Strange requests
As though you were
My mother's breath.

That curve describes
My mind's fall away
From why I love you.
I just take the
Curves in my mind
And love you anyway.

"VICTORY!" Flash on
That, and your teeth
Shining out at me
From every pore.
Always smiling and
Going home again.

If I manage to live
Without you or my
Mother, it's because
I never turn around
But find you there.

I NEED TO SEE YOU LIKE THAT

to remember my name is not MIKE
but several club footed tones
of a special grave we have
for those who come apart first
fill up the words later.

Suck my eyes. Suck my eyes!
Bar full of blinds can't you see
I'm eating up your sadness in
that glass container you
introduced to everyone as
your new friend?

Believe me, no one likes a masochist
the way you do. Only I don't ever
want to hurt again, or hurt never again
too much inside the way love makes me do
when we call it love at first night.

This isn't fair. I know that.
What it is is fairheaded like light bulbs
that don't work or workmen who don't
saunter to lunch and then hard eye
the women walking by as though they were
all chickens in the first Sunday meal
and you weren't sure whether to feel good
about so much meat or nervous because
you knew it when it was alive.

There is no time left for the way
you like to see the breasts of trees
shine out in all accidents above
the muted metal of some deformed idea
of communication we call speed.

Forget the eyes and hands just
concentrate on the breath Buddy
and remember what the Buddhists say:
Shut up and sit! Or was it
Sit up and shut . . .

THE WAY IT FEELS NOW

you all stand there
wait for me to answer
I forget the question
as usual you remind me

If I could keep up this pace
I could write my novel tonite
or fuck up my typewriter with
jammed keys from moving my two
fingers too fast but it would
never be fast enough for my
thoughts which are never fast
enough for my feelings which
is why I'm always in trouble
with the people I love by the
time I begin to think I dont
love them anymore

ALMOST A MONTH WITHOUT WRITING A POEM

well
these past few weeks have been memorable
as I waited
for my life to blossom like my feet and hands did
once
inside my mother
but it only went on humming like a motor waiting
for a new use
or user

FEELING

tight and angled
like a 17th century woodcut
only in my veins
where I rarely imagine myself
or anything recognizably me
because blood has always seemed so
impersonal and uninteresting
unlike shoulders or fur coats or
new things to do with skin and bodies.

I love the way a fortune hunter
sucks his brandy without venom
after the wealthy prey has gone away
and wonder why I envy such classic guts
because it takes more than simple moxy
to have passionate sex by proxy
or are there people who can come
at the thought of a thousand dollar bill
the way some can at the image of a gun?

I wonder what ever happened to
post-war-morality and when
will we see what was generating
the light at the end of the tunnel
or was it a funnel?

LISTS
for Deb Fredo

coverage of vernacular
deep image like say:

the dead end in the soap

or

super rabbits of the sleep in my veins

no more graphs
no more stories
no more apoplexy

just: the highway of your frame
      the lush thigh of her brown eye
      the cruising speed of orange clouds
      the boys and girls in each xerox copier

o Walt Whitman, great housewife of American lust
you gave us the lists to improve upon
and now we wait to find out who will
or if
making our own for purely personal pleasure
as the solitary lover explains her hands
or the invalid his routines

(nobody has to be insulted though)

TOUCH

touch has asked me to
memorize your sweet smell

"FAG HAG"

SHE comes across into sky face up
queen of bookkeeping and soft asses
she touches yours and his together
teeth gleam and no one has smiled
between the two of you she glows
I love her
because I don't know what I feel
or what they want
when they put their so sure fingers
to my cheek and show me teeth
I think of burning at the stake
or inheriting millions

1974

"I want to find out what new mind I'm using.
 Why does it come here
 where it has never thought of before?"

-Nathan Whiting Distancing

FEELING GOOD TED
for Ted Berrigan

being alone
thinking of you
how much more you do for me
what you thought Whalen did
for you and should do for anyone
who "knew" and I just didnt know
then how much it all meant to me
being "a poet" and growing older
all alone in the middle of court
half hustler because we
or at least me
so often feel uncomfortable
in the world
in other people's beds
in other people
sometimes
but mostly in ourselves
until those bright spots
leave us "feeling good"
like right now, tonight
here alone for the first time
in my first apartment by myself
since I split my home in 1960
to go be the baddest jazz musician
the white world had ever offered to
the black world
"go Jim Dandy!"
and now I just feel fine growing older
alone but not by myself
because I always have you to read
or Sylvia to look at on my wall
or Love Unlimited on the radio
all them others who went out to star
and did

enough to keep me from dying
enough to keep me still wanting to star
still starring

FELT

what is it supposed to come from *me!!*
me from!
burning mother fucker
light lightly
         introducing:
what from!!
you "focking beetches"
you "focking basturds"
feel it
like vomit on the screen
we refuse to suspend belief for!
what fucking flaming wall we climbed!
you climb it!!!
reduce this to this mother fucker tip
tipping lightly
introducing the mother of this fucker
who tips *her!*
what is coming from *her!!!*
what is coming *for* her!!!
license to vomit babies
that we refuse to be touched
turn around and frown
all the bastards fucking
inside it's taking over the body
taking over the tastes of insides
taste from where!!
me taste what!!
refuse to taste!!
refuse to be controlled by "taste"!!!
taste lightly curling the wall's tongue
what tongue from *me!!!*
taste fucking you vomit baby!!!
let refuse taste vomit you inside fucker!!
no tasting
introduce what is supposed to be me

mother
wall
insides
touch
vomit
fucking

ART
for Ramon Osuna

Art come to homes
from far away.

It is sent out from
The Power House.

Big Dealers
are in
The Power House.

These Dealers
send out Art
for people to use.

Great waves go out
from The Power House.

Art
rides on these waves.

The great waves
take Art
to cities
and suburbs.

They take the Art
that helps people
in these places
to live better.

The waves take
        Art
to Your Town.

TWO STORIES

1. i cant write about it

2. i cant talk about it

PEOPLE

I used to say "my people"
when I meant some

the woman Goldie Hawn
was trying to be and
was in "Sugarland Express"
and then the black dude
with the little black boy
maybe two years old flinching
and crying as the dude
kept commanding him closer
and he stopped in baby shoes
to get his ass whipped
for something we couldnt
know about just passing
by on the street like that
and Terry saying "thats
something I learned, dont
ever interfere with people
and their kids, even the cops
cant do anything about it"
but things've changed since
Terry learned that, I tried
to believe, as we walked on
feeling white and alike in
our hatred of violence
I kept thinking of my son
how vulnerable he seems to me
and what might happen to him
learning things like that
poor boy was learning so early

at the block party people
pushed me aside worse than cops
at demonstrations and it was

just young black kids not
polite enough to walk around
or say excuse me or notice

I used to say "people"
when I meant everybody

FALLING IN LOVE

"trying to catch my breath"
makes a lot of sense as an
expression having to do with
"took my breath away"
because you did this morning
with your mellower than me
appearance meaning eyes and
the way your clothes seemed
to be around you not on you
and your skin a light for
the way your body was reading
the atmosphere casually as
you passed through it picking
out fruit and some kind of oil
that sounded healthy and
filled your pint jar and
the name of it filled your
mouth as you spoke to me
for the first time answering
a question I wanted to sound
like "breathless" in spirit
but not in will because I am
always afraid my frightened
teenage punk will look out
from this adult mature hungry
thirty-two-year-old frame of
mine that reminds me of all
I've been through till now
without you and how cool the
air would have been in Jersey
summers with you around to
fill it and then somehow I
mentioned my kids and became
afraid that that would sound
like a complicated set of
circumstances for you to move

in without losing some of the
my god it's not even the usual
sexuality or sensuality or
fun-of-another-body feeling
but something more like I
dreamt in grammar school when
the possibility of love began
to take shape more in dreams
than in watching the girls on
their way home from school or
not playing ball with us in
the playground where I know
now you could easily outpitch
me or any of the other punks
I grew up with who were as
nervous as I was about how
foolish we might all really be
and tried making that go away
with our fists so that I was
"trying to catch my breath"
even when I wasnt falling in love

YOU
for Terence Winch

yeah, I miss you
what else is new

I'm not strong
but when I need to be strong
people see me being strong
and I'm strong then
for them

I got along nicely without you
I got along pretty well with you too
I missed you
but I kept busy with everyone else
you left behind missing you too
but not as much as they would if
I wasnt there to distract them
tell them what they wanted to do
do it for them

sometimes I got angry at you
not without loving you
missing you
wishing you were here
realizing it wasnt anything you
or I could change
but still feeling mad about it
the way you could go away
the way you could have to go away
I never had to go away
I just went away anyway
and it would change everything
just like I wanted it to
but nothing would be different
and I'd know it was just a whim
not necessity

like it was for you
or so many others
with me it's always been whimsy
no one would ever call me that
whimsical
so maybe it's not true after all
maybe I'm more like you than we knew

when you get back
it'll all be changed again you know
nothing will ever be the same
except we'll do a lot of the same things
we'll know a lot of the same people
we'll push ourselves around the same old
circles and squares
we'll have a lot of fun together
and there wont be anyone like us
again
there never was
what else is new
I miss you

FATHERS DAY

The suffering in 1942 as Spring
breaks open my mother for me.
In Europe the Jews, the Communists,
the Queers, the proud and
loving Rom are brutalized
again. The Irish in me is
emphasized, not the German,
not the Gypsy
I hope is there.

"You cant write books" my father said
before I did, and after. At 75
me 32 he warns "Raise your children
right, get them through college
okay, then you can write your books."

He knows a lot I dont. I know
a lot he never thought of. We share
little of that, though we share a lot.
Not much through words, but gestures
and the looks of him I carry always.
We are afraid of each other
like con men, or lovers, we know
we can hurt.

WHAT WE'RE MISSING

Old corny 40s style music takes me back
I was a kid
after "the war"
older sisters and brothers digging 78 records
no tv
radio fights, like Joe Louis and Ezzard Charles
somehow the seasons seemed more like seasons
less like semesters or election years or crises
things werent easy
but things werent impossible
growing up was a drag
but it really hadnt started yet
that was the 50s
this was the 40s
I was still a kid
life was still a gift I didnt have to work for
all this and it's 1974.

What music can do for us
we should be able to do for ourselves
and sometimes we do,
when that happens too often they put us away
or try to change us,
when it happens just enough
and we learn how to share it
they make us stars,
when it doesnt happen enough
but enough to let us know it's there and possible
we fight with it and with too many other things
blaming almost everything, anything,
coming close to being fools, but not crazy,
or geniuses, eccentrics, but not stars,
failures, but not magnificent,
or almost failures.

When it doesnt happen at all
we dont know what we're missing.

1975

"It's always night or we wouldn't need light."

-Thelonious Monk

NEW YEARS DAY POEM 1975

According to my Ma, god rest her soul,
whatever you're doin on New Years Eve
you'll be doin the whole new year long.
This New Years Eve I was on my way back
from taking my kids to New Jersey
to see their four aunts and four uncles
and twelve cousins and grandpop
who asked me if I was renting rooms out.
I said no, of course not, I live by myself
in an "efficiency apartment." He said,
well when I called down there on Christmas
morning you werent in but some woman was.
We watched the Pittsburgh-Oakland game
together, my dad and me. The woman
and me watched the Pasadena Tournament
of Roses Parade this morning and
the theme was the American Heritage
like Bo Decker who had his picture in *Life*
magazine because he was a champion
professional rodeo rider or O'Lyn Callahan
on the Yamaha Organ "playing with the
light jazz style popularized by the
Carpenters, but with the depth of sound
heard in a Count Basie big-band recording,"
or the annual family and neighborhood reunion
sponsored by the Farradays who lived
next door to us where I grew up, they had
nine children, the father drank and was
on "relief" as we called welfare back then,
the mother was a five-by-five supermarket
cashier, the oldest girl and oldest boy
seemed laid back and normal but the rest
went bananas, one girl ran away to
Hollywood, one boy named Joe to Hawaii
where he got a good job in a bank and
a wealthy lover named Jim who was found

murdered one day and Joe became the
prime suspect especially when the will
was read and all Jim's money was suddenly
Joe's, Jim's family contested it
but Joe got off, married a Hawaiian girl,
built a house for her in Florida and
one next door for his mom but after only
a few weeks the girl went back to Hawaii
where Joe also went to an even better
job with an even better bank, while
his brother Donald tried to hold up
a California bank in drag and was caught
and sent to Leavenworth but is out now
with his bleached blonde hair and fights
with his sister Carrie the toughest in
the clan who was the first employee
of Spartan's Mill to make management
and not be a member of the Spartan family,
it was rumored the oldest Spartan boy
had eyes for her until she got drunk
at an office Christmas party and made
a pass at one of his female secretaries,
he fired her on the spot while another
brother Lou, the one my age, married well,
his father-in-law was president of
the bank Lou later was caught embezzling
from, he didnt have to go to jail like
Donald. My family was the other end
of the spectrum, righteous and rich for
the neighborhood at the time, full of
cops and priests and people who said
the rosary every evening around the
television set turned off for fifteen
minutes of prayer because the family
that prays together stays together and
we did, landing not in jail or deviant
relationships but in the way we fought
ourselves from combining beauty and

114

talent with education so that our
performances would bring raves from
the critics and it would be said:
we have everything going for us! like
everyone thought we did, whereas
the Farradays had little or nothing
going for them but still bring it all
back together for 15.60 a person
each summer at some catering joint
on the hill, where one of us had our
wedding reception and I drank soda
cause I had to quit drinking like
my father did and my youngest sister
has finally done, the others looped
each evening dreaming of bombs that
blow it all away, the growing blindness
of my oldest sister, her two adopted
daughters guiding her and pestering her,
her cop husband who my father always
said had never set foot on a train
or in a restaurant until he married
into our family, or my brother the
ex-cop and present postmaster asking
how could I see myself as so Irish,
not just plain American, but how proud
he is that his oldest daughter intends
to marry a boy named Doyle, who
wisely declined the invitation to watch
the Rams-Vikings game with us, my brother
reprimanding me for saying shit when
the ref made a bad call reminding me
there were women nearby, almost
crying later in the day when the Raiders
lost, like he almost cried when fifteen
years ago I wanted to marry a black girl
and he was just a rookie patrolman
getting headaches from the way
neighborhood people looked at him for

being my brother, if he only knew
that five years before that the youngest
Farraday, Dale, who now sells cars
in his father-in-law's lot, pulled
my peter till it squirted in the bushes
and when we were through I pulled him
up to me by the front of his shirt
and told him I'd break his fucking legs
so he'd never dance the rest of his life
if he ever told anyone about what
we'd done and now I'm blasting it
all over the poetry world losing
the universal appeal that's made me
such a shining success, or was it
chanteuse, my story, like yours,
a mixture of brag heartache bluster
and the funniest tough love affair
ever put on stage screen or in St. Marks
Church, o mama I got the fucking flu
so bad I want to die, I wish you were
alive to tell me something soothing
like never put your hat on the bed
it's bad luck, that's what people
used to say about me, and some of
the Farradays, Fran Farraday became
a mailman but got fired when they found
half the mail in the back of his car
instead of in folks hands and heads
and little letter boxes sitting on
the colored tv for the husband to see
when he comes in from a hard days work
to find his wife shining her tits and
kids playing if the shit fits wear it,
and it always fits, like holiday greetings,
my saying to you: happy new year, I
hope you never catch this goddamn flu.

POEM SPRING 1975

I lean into the future these days

smell my children stretching into theirs

like my fingers the first time I touched a woman there

get off my back

white man's burden —

guilt and anxiety

and white man's burden's burden:

self-righteousness

what happened

I stopped writing poetry

started writing pornography

and made more money at poetry

this is the way institutions develop

not writers

I'D LIKE TO WRITE A POEM TO SPRING

shit, I'd like to write anything

DRY SPELLS

nothing comes
nothing goes
everybody asks
whats the matter
you say
nothing

it's like
living without ego
how can those bliss heads
get anything done
you dont really ask yourself
because you dont really care

it's like giving up exercising
& your body stays in shape
or taking up exercising &
it doesnt

it's like pounding a nail
into a hollow plaster wall
or getting someone to admit
theyre wrong after you realize
it doesnt matter

it's like running out of
fantasies when you're fucking
& dont want to be

it's like falling asleep
in a dream
& waking up
still believing you
never dream

1976

"Everything should be as simple as it *can* be,
  Says Einstein,
  But not simpler."

                              -Louis Zukofsky *"A"*

2/4/76

I used to want to be
a nice tough guy

Now I want to be
a tough nice guy

ESSAY ON THE STATE OF POETRY
Winter 75-76 NYC

First arguments should be above principle.
One should not display bad taste and a lack of basic manners
before noncreators.
There is not "only one kind" of poetry; there are two.
There exists a tacit understanding between the author and the
reader by which the former calls herself the nurse and accepts
the latter as patient.
It is humankind who consoles the poet! The roles cant be re-
versed at will.
Poetry is not a mountain, still less a peak. It is an awesome
and fertile valley.
There are words like those of an idea, dreaminess of life, wordy
way, the preposition "of", the disorganized step, which have
allowed to infiltrate into our heads a poetry languorous with
poseurs, like "nothingness". To pass from movement to dance
when one is asleep takes but a single dream.

The perturbances, aurealities, contrivances, exceptions to the
sexual or bionic lure, the body of positivism, the
lunaties, willful arbitrariness, tantrums, constructions, over
views, camps, jealousies, elitisms, nearsighted innovations,
movies, structured occurrences, things which should be left done,
the cinematic prospects of the obvious stranger who eyeballs
the genitals of some living illusion, elegant and graceful ex-
periences, surfaces treated with a shell-like "being", the over
whelming obsession with professionalism, strange faeces that the
contributor would prefer not to acknowledge, the inoculation with
dope stupors, betternesses, Venuses, irrational grins, cultivated
neuroses, the channel-filled-circuits down which one forces
imagination at bay, exonerations, lack of ancestory,
packed phrases, subtleness, looms, fucks worse than suicides,
the coterie of poets turned novelists, strategies, loads, her
stories, perceptual extremes, reason whittled on with
immunity, the dours of set bitches, androgynes, tough guys, tough
guy ladies, simpletons, freaks, the hip, the aloof, the hours

124

dunked in tv despondency, the jerks, the corruptions, that which
is inflective like a child, that intellectual desolation,
stoned ulcers, hips like fire hydrants, the exercises of
a writer who takes the escalator up the slope of opportunities
and scorns his rivals with facile indifference, dislocations,
chumpings, the innumerable elisions . . .
is it time at last to react against that which only amuses us or
wows us around so deliberately?

"MY FIGHT"

All I ever wanted to do was be in love. That's the first memory,
that feeling, longing, to be inside the bigger longing and the satis-
faction it could overwhelm me with when a beautiful pair of eyes
looked back at mine, even at four or five, and meant something
secret and sexy and way beyond anything just growing up would
ever teach me, I knew it already for that moment, and knew it was
"love" and wanted to always feel that way. So I spent as much of
my time as I could trying to be in love and being in love. School
was easy, after school wasnt, boys wanting to fight, girls wanting
to make fun of the vulnerability of boys wanting only to love,
and all that classic stuff. Well, I've been in love more of my thirty-
four years than I havent been and the only thing I'd want different
is to be and have been in love for all of it and as much of it as could
fill me and envelop me and enlighten my understanding of pleasure
and joy without taking me away forever.

NOTICE TO CREDITORS

I hate to make the connections
all evident and intelligible
and consistently directed and
informed — *references* and this
from this and "it" excised for
the creation of categories to then
be studied for relationships to be
applied to forging continuous logic
of structures — institutions — and
justifying claims to overlapping
areas of interest and conquest
and contradicting claims of priorities
and resolutions to no conclusion
other than "holding back the void" —

head in hands —heavy — just from
servicing the day — and the sky
so blue it's worth a ritual or two —
at least a relaxation toward a
culminating smile of recognition —
(i.e. acceptance of the cosmic
totality of which we (you/me)
are such an integral portion —
e.g. the smile as reflection of
the blue — the blue of course
reflection of the logical extension
of *total association* —unlike
"free association's" limitations
of perception as in only an
elite of imaginative expertise
of which I readily admit I am
a member can perceive — but
it's *work* — the rest is "natural" —

"it" isn't "poetry" *(NO IMAGES!)*
"it" does not equal "poetry"
"it" does not become and is not
becoming "poetry" — "Eddie!"
"Yeah!?" — "Hah?!" — "Yeah!?" —

NEW PROSE NOSTALGIA
for Ray DiPalma, Ted Greenwald,
*   Edmund White, and Bruce Andrews*

Am I that smart. Do I like to be derivative. Did I choose to be.
If I did why did I. What *is* wrong with that anyway. Is it like
shoveling snow in June. Or just the sound of shovel on sidewalk.
Not like the sibilants of s's at all, rather like that "rather" in
one of *my* sentences. Not: are my eyes so bad I can't read the
subway signs; or why does that hand-me-down sweater seem so
special. Do we love the family we remember more than the
family we know. (What if she were to come through the door
right now — would it change anything: stop or start something
as personal as (would a phone call — interruption — resolve all
this) this is. Maybe I should wake her, tell her to call her, call
him myself, apologize, explain, emote, win over, just say I'm
overwhelmed, still overwhelmed. Would that get me anywhere.
Is that what I want — to get somewhere. Where. Where there
is no need to be appreciated for accomplishments never
fulfilled, compliments never filled. Are the visual arts less
restrictive. Does it matter, I mean would there be any choice
anyway. Why not let the limitations define the structure for
us. Is that really what it's all about. And if it is do the ones
with the most limitations find it any easier, or more intense.
How helpful is a limitation like having "it" and "thing" for
favorite words as opposed to "dark" or "baleful" or"double"
or "breakdown" or the most prized words of a prize-winning
poet. Is it true Yeats's advice to younger poets and playwrights
was a list of words never to use like "mountain" or "sward."

What if all the words I shouldn't use I already don't. Would it
help to make a list of words I should try to use. Is it enough
to know what to avoid in images, like talking stones/silent
accusing stones, or fish with feathers/birds with fins, etc. What
if instead of "terrific" or "boring" your favorite qualifier is
"etc." Can concern for language make you unfit for employ-
ment, a late riser, an indifferent lover, a schemer, a fop. "Fop
breakdown rather dark, double dark like the feathers of stones,
the fins on talking poets." Will all the poets and writers working
in schools destroy the glamour of secret self-righteous aware-
ness. Kids treading on each other's right to lonely glory, long
range revenge. Is it possible to even seriously discuss the creative
output of children. Are choices made in public ever valid. Do
consequences determine actions. Is memory creative. Can
exercises exercise the time in which they exist. In other words,
is the life span, or life expectancy, of an exercise determined
by — especially interesting is the question of interruptions and
their influence on supposedly inherently self-contained struc-
tures. How often can you use a "v" word, as opposed to a "c"
or "s" or "i" or "t" word. Is anything natural, or everything.
If all writing is originally artificial is the effect of all writing
equally artificial. If not, why not. Are all the possible answers
to the preceding question definitions of structure, or reasons
why structure is essential. Does structure determine effect.
If not, why not. Are the answers to that preceding question
the explanations for style, therefore qualifying effect as
dependent on taste. Or is taste determined by style. Would
someone shouting in your window be more distracting than the
130

sound of your telephone ringing. Right now maybe you could care less (there's someone using the shower and you need to urinate — how does that compare with there's someone taking a shower and you need to take a piss). Is the "someone" used in relation to the "I" we began with any more or less vague than the "someone" used in relation to the "you" we have evolved to. Can writing in longhand (any relation to the weaponry term "shortarm") create parallels in syle for all who do so. Is this derivative of writers I've never read if it sounds like their style, or do you have to prove I read them first. Is being smart, or smarter, a matter of style. Is style another product of original sin. Was original sin arbitrary or original since there was no one else to blame at the time. Is blame a matter of religion. Is religion irrelevant to style. Is the trend toward vowels or consonants. Are either inherently reactionary. If so, facto. Why can some artists, writers, and performers accomplish serious ends through silly means while others seem silly no matter what the means, or less silly than stupid. Is stupidity a matter of style. Is there any sure method for determining intelligence except for the articulation of it. Or is that only a measure of the quality of manipulation of it. Is manipulation a measure of intelligence. Is manipulation always only a means to an end even if that end is to demonstrate the degree of manipulation. Are generalities always manipulations. Is language always manipulative. Are specifics — naming names especially — any more informative than non-specifics or is that a matter of style. Stylistics. I'm surprised there was never a group called "The Specifics," but not surprised there has been no humorous,

but serious of intent, critical study of men in the arts written
by a woman. But can I imagine both as interesting additions
to a world I might be running. Is all creation an expression
of the need to run something or someone. Or is all imagina-
tion an expression of the need to run something or someone.
Can you imagine a book of "Collected Runnings" or a retro-
spective exhibit of an artist's runnings. Is it too stupid or really
just unpleasant sounding. I seem to have totally mismanaged
my life. Is that more unpleasant. Can we equate "managing"
with "running." If I haven't "totally" mismanaged my life,
"misrun" it, I can still feel for any given length of time, until
I realize otherwise, perhaps as a result of specifics, intelligence,
structure, interruption, style, etc. as though I have so far.
Realizing I haven't "totally" mismanaged it doesn't relieve
me any. Is that because the degree of mismanagement doesn't
matter during periods of mismanagement or the effects of them.
Is eating not an interruption because we usually "manage" it.
Should criticism be more specific than this. Is this an essay.
What if this were a sestina written out as prose. Would it be
any easier to understand. Is that the key to structure. (my
eyes hurt, I have to stop, I used to be attractive most of the
time, even when I just got out of bed, is that age or a simple
matter of hair stylists and choosing the right ones — "Beep
beep" doesn't sound like any horn I ever heard.

1977

"You are what you look for"

-Ronald Johnson *Eyes & Objects*

ODE TO MANHATTAN

O — city escaping the air
it isnt love I feel for you
exactly — at least right now —
it's more like the possibility-of-
love which perhaps is greater
than the-first-realization-
of-love which is certainly
better than this-is-love-alright
which we all know/but hate
to admit outdoes
looks-like-love-is-here-to-stay

O — I'm here to stay
at least for the moment — and you —
you overgrown medieval
market place are obviously
staying come what may — and
maybe that's the basis of all
I feel for you and feel
you return — our tenacity —
is there a little too
much self-credit in that term —
our willingness to let the
possibilities keep us alive even
when the probabilities and
unavoidable outcomes seem to be
killing us

        I mean
O city — you give me that old
maybe-it-isnt-love-or-
what-first-excites-us-in-that-
word-but-it's-keeping-us-alive-
and-hoping-anyway feeling
and I'm glad to have it back

YOU CAN'T TRUST ANYBODY

of course
but
you have to

4 APRIL 77
for Ed Cox

I can hear the rain
on the skylight
the casement windows
metal and glass
that's lasted
this long (at least
100 years — more)
what's in store
for me & mine
the next 100 — it —
the rain — makes
me wonder & feel
secure at once —
it's the energy
that connects me
to all who've
come before —
(sitting in their shelters
feeling safe from the
wet and nasty damp
still damp — some
leaks — but not *"in"*
it — the rain — & not
"out of it" because
it's there making
its presence felt just
above the head on
the roof — my son
in bed — me soon —
to fall asleep to
that music — the
true music of the
spheres — the atmo
spheres — & there's
always more where
that came from

AMERICAN SNAPSHOTS

In snapshot tries I
send you home to Kodak
& be amused alone & adult
with the wicked safety unlatched

I mean I cant make it to your reading
& I dont want to & I dont know why
is it because you never said anything
to me that wasnt ultimately about you
& your concerns & like every other poet
I know I'm an egocentric pain in the ass
too but that doesnt excuse you
or the rest of them
the rest of them Hah
more poets than politicians now
and more politicians than cops
and more cops than teachers
and more teachers than schools
and more schools than museums
and more museums than lakes
and more lakes than earnest do-gooders
and more earnest do-gooders than good meals in restaurants
and more good meals in restaurants than meat in hot dogs
and more meat in hot dogs than nutrition
and more nutrition than new ideas
what a time to be alive & alone
amused with snapshot attempts
to keep yourself content
with nothing I can do
except play dangerous

"TELEPATHY OF WIRES"
for Hart Crane

A column of "ofs" supporting the ceiling
at which point every aspiration collides
with its limitations in this domesticity
of space and atmosphere according to our
own perceptions of environmental custody

the basis for the column of "ofs" within
which support is surrounded and embraced
by every desirous invocation of similar
forces of control over what waits alone
for us and the resolutions we initiated

BLESSED ARE THE B-B-B-B-B
for Ray DiPalma

This far bought out of size
we shaped intelligently
according to our youthful beauty of thought
the plodding insistence of our brain songs
that this and that could bring us home
to where the intellect and street sense are
not compromised by stepn fetchit punk sellouts
tough enough to sell themselves short and
ambitious enough to figure out who's buying.
We can't abide that blithe shit on the shoes
of our coming this far without
we go to meet them with only our fucking
language and the heads, our worlds, too
full, various, divergent to be easy
to support as if we didn't know
and that knowledge wasn't the cornerstone
of the art we made new where they
make now, okay too but not
even mortal like ours, so
timely and historically news is theirs
they seem like stars only just labeled
while we seem to them a reflection of
the same old moon, only
that's not the moonlight that's
the night we first felt our rage
and knew our storm was poetry.

ART OF GLASS
for Nick Muska

He writes that one of the attractions of Toledo
is a place where they make glass
as well as the local rhythm and blues, the "jazz"
that made "My Life" a cliche before it spawned
a new life for the art of class busting
which in the late 50s was survival but now on the eve of the 80s
isn't much to shout about unless
you're a cultural journalist out of things to say
and afraid of those who aren't but
you live in Toledo, San Diego, St. Paul
and the dumb things in life are too much with
the things you wish to transcend, escape, over-
whelm with your easy courage not so easily expressed
so when you see it anywhere you don't care
what the cognoscenti have to do with the cossacks
who think the waves they ride inevitably reach shore
where the good but creative life awaits them, only
what's more fulfilling than to figure out
what's making waves in you and riding out to meet them
before they're due — or casting them in glass
the wave, the sea which gives it substance, and
the shore which gives it class

1978

"It's hard to be easy."

-Ned Rorem *An Absolute Gift*

SNOW 2

It *is* a planet,
the atmosphere
always alien
except when we
make a metaphor
for our growth
& death out of
it: "O look it's
a beautiful blue
sky this morning
and it snowed
last night and
the snow is so
bright and shiny
in the sunlight —
what a great day!"
beauty being a
condition we re-
quire for our
happiness not to
exist but to
unfold as though
growing older we
contribute some-
how to it, perhaps
through our obser-
vations, or our
naming & recording
of it, or maybe
just by pretending
it isn't another
world.

THE COLD

You know what that's been like
These winters
Remember the winter of '77
'78 is already worse
Fuck the pioneers
They had it rough on purpose
We didnt intend this shit
We meant to be the future
Where the choices were unlimited
And all good
But no
It's the same old same old
Here's your three choices
The first two stink and the last one
Well we all know about the last one
That's the one where you think you
Have a chance
Only the chance is
Your last one

Goddamn it's so fucking cold

EXPLA-NA-NA-NA-NA-NA
for A.L.

Do we need to balk at
talk of "signs" and the
signified in the eyes of
a "relationship" that is
not the one/one/one/one
of them though only not
full of mistakes and the
cautious minority of sex
in its evidentiary con-
text like knowing where
we are in a room without
going or coming together?

I love you kid, and I ex-
pect the same but don't
demand it cause it goes
around anyway, and with
you it's not desperate
though that leaves us
without the passionate
basis for jealous strong-
holds of the emotive pro-
cesses known to the 1970s
as tough but romantic ob-
sessiveness — beat/beat
and all that other stuff
we retreat from when you
understand my history as
the necessary extension
of my skin and organs and
means of transmitting all
that to you without ever
intending a coup or coup-
ling beyond what we have.

147

And what we have is not in
the way of whatever else
we need and desire and use
to approve ourselves and
the ways we move forward
without going away, I mean
unless I'm not doing enough
in which case whatever it
is I'm falling short of is
somebody else's move or
storage cause this is all
I have right now and it's
not unkind to me, or what
I feel for you. That's love
too, only less demanding.

If I talk too much it's only
too much out there, in here
it's who I am and how I know it.

1978 ALMOST SPRING
AND I'M STILL AFRAID
OF ALMOST EVERYTHING

what success might bring
and not bring, what I
think I am and am not,
what others think of me
or don't think, what I
did and what I do and
what I forgot and never
knew and what I remember
and force on you as too
much of me, what I see and
fail to see, what I might
do with you or without
you and what you might
see I don't see or be I
can't be or want to de-
liver that I can't accept
or expect from me that I
haven't got or don't know
how to give or don't want
to or shouldn't or should
I, decisions, and fate
and not being able to
sleep, too much dope, not
enough money, no home for
long enough to relax, no
community that accepts me
the way I accept myself
when I do, the times I
don't, where I want to be
but don't see anywhere
when I get there which is
always less once I'm in
it cause otherwise what
would I be doing there,

getting down on myself,
getting down on others,
thinking I'm so much more
than I might be or more
than so many others I don't
even know, them, everyone,
myself, you, the changing
weather and what it might
do, keep me in, make me
restless, the jobs, the
assignments, the writing
left to do, the writing
done so long ago and only
now paid attention to,
misleading, being mis-
understood, letting go,
hanging on, my private
insanity, my public
eccentricity, being a
jerk, being a maniac,
being ordinary, being
less than I expect and
more than I accept and
being left.

MOTHER'S DAY 1978

It's raining
like Good Friday
or so we believed
when we were kids
that somehow the
weather reflected
our Catholic faith
& honored the death
of the Son of God
with rain or at least
clouds and greyness
and this the day my
mother died 12 years
ago when I was 24
& thought myself too
old to feel too alone
with the passing of
someone I rarely saw
and was afraid to let
know me too well but
felt amazingly intimate
with nonetheless because
she was a woman and I
loved women and knew
that between her thighs
out of the place I loved
most to be I had once
been for the first time
going the other direction
out into the world she
seemed so able to maintain
her innocence in, even
after seven kids, an
alcoholic husband all
the deaths big families
live through and even

151

the crazy betrayals of
her standards and beliefs
by her baby who didnt
come around much anymore
but was there by her side
when the struggle with
whatever came to take her
began and she called out
for her oldest the priest
and for her baby who rose
to take her hand and let
her see he was there but
her eyes showed fear and
anger and confusion at what
I was sure she took to be
a stranger because of the
beard that was just another
sign of my estrangement
from these people who had
once thought I would be
some kind of answer to
the questions that the
future perplexed them with
constantly these days
only instead I grew away
from them and on my returns
always disturbed them with
my latest alteration in
my movement toward knowing
what I might be as well as
what I had been and them
and when the nurse came in
to turn off the machines
and their ominous low hum
that graphically displayed
my mother's loss to whatever
it was that had frightened
her so, I felt so fucking bad

for adding to that loss with
my stupid disguise that when
we got home, 3AM on Mother's
Day 1966 to tell our father
the news I left my brothers
and sisters and in-laws to
shave off the mask to discover
the skin beneath the months'
old growth of hair as tender
as a baby's, my chin my
cheeks the skin around my
lips all soft and white and
delicate like a lady's, a
side I was yet to discover
for myself all I knew then
was I would never let that
disguise hide me from the
world I had yet to realize
I understood more from her
sure knowledge passed on to
the child I had been than all
the books and experiences and
hip friends I had gone to since
but when I came downstairs they
all thought I had done it for
him and were grateful I had
been thoughtful of those left
behind especially he who had
taught us most of what we knew
about life it seemed to them
though without her he might
have been the narrowminded
crank he sometimes was although
he too knew how to use his
emotions to understand and that
must have been what brought them
together or perhaps what kept
them there but even in death

the nature of their relationship
took on the security of her care
as the oldest sister read the
note found in the hospital
drawer with her personal stuff
letting us know she knew what
we had only half suspected that
this was it and we'd be left
without that spiritual wisdom
she had offered unwittingly as
she spoke to us once again when
my sister read where daddy's
medicine could be found and what
dosages he should take and where
she'd left the newly cleaned
shorts and shirts and how he
liked his meals and when and
who should remember to take
their insulin and who among
all these children who were so
long since grown and running
homes of their own but still
so near and dependent on her
she understood in the guts that
were half gone and caused the
heart to close down she knew
they needed to know she'd
never be gone for good but
was only giving advice from
another home the one she had
convinced them could be theirs
because it had always been hers
and now she was there waiting
once again for her babies to
bring their confusion and fear
and strangeness in a world so
far removed from what their
world had given them she was
154

that world more than any son
of god could ever have been
but she left them to him anyway
despite the reality I saw in
her eyes when whatever it was
came to take her from inside
it wasn't any meek and loving
lord unless she took him for
some fearsome stranger too as
she had me and I had her for
all the years I never knew how
much I owed her just for never
giving in but always giving . . .

LOVING WOMEN

In 1956 I got on a number 31 bus
in Vailsburg, the last neighborhood
in Newark before South Orange where
I was going home to, after spending
the hours after school with a girl
I'd just met and fallen in love with.

It was a beautiful spring evening,
around six thirty and I was late for
dinner as well as playing hooky from
an after school job, so I knew I was
on my way to an argument with my
father, who would be waiting angrily.

The bus was full of old ladies and
only a few men, stragglers from their
jobs in Newark — but no kids, just
me, 14, and so thin I thought it was
embarrassing most of the time, only
this time I knew it was sexy and great.

My shirt was unbuttoned down to the
fifth buttonhole and my hairless
teenaged chest was exposed enough
to see that right between my little
male tits was the imprint of two
bright red lips — a lipstick tattoo.

It almost glowed the way I flaunted
it, showed them all what I'd been up
to and was proud of, proud to be a
teenager when that word was only one
step removed from monster or moron,
criminal or alien being — or love.

The old ladies stared, some sternly,
some jealously, only one smiling,
approvingly, she was tougher looking
than the rest, like an alcoholic
aunt who smoked too much but her
eyes shone from few regrets and me.

I was a punk, a juvenile delinquent,
and a total enigma to my parents and
older brothers and sisters, but I was
a hero to my dreams and only on rare
occasions like this one did I live up
to them — swaggering down the aisle.

When I took my seat the bright eyed
lady turned to take another look and
caught me sniffing the fingers of my
right hand that had just been where
I longed all day and night to be, to
worship in, to build my temple there.

I'd start my own religion in that
mysterious church defined by the
lines formed first by the knees and
calves of the starlets who perched
on the railings of ocean liners for
the cameras of *The Daily Mirror* or

The Daily News, their skirts pulled
up to cap their knees like an exotic
hood under which the rest caressed
itself so obviously and promised
the answer to everything I had always
wanted to know — back there, somewhere

between what I could only imagine
despite all I'd seen in short shorts
and girly magazines, because this was
news, the real life beauties posing
before going off with some lucky dude
I might someday be. Only I knew I

didn't have to wait to find out, I
found out every chance I could get
or make and still I didn't know and
longed to know and owed it all to
that crazy haven for my frustration
and confusion with the times and the

values I couldn't share and didn't care
about outside the trouble they caused
me every fucking day. The lady knew
what I was doing, what I was smelling
on my fingers to make me forget the
inevitable limitations, this far and

no farther, 1956 after all and an Irish
Catholic girl, like my sisters and
cousins and nieces, only poorer, without
even a phone so when I got home I would
have to satisfy myself the rest of the
night with my fingers brushing my lips

and unshaved fine hairs beneath my
nose that alone could put me in touch
with this beautiful girl from Vailsburg.
All through dinner the reverbs from
arguing kept the place silent or phony
until my father, not noticing how often

I wiped my mouth, got to feeling better
with the dinner and the evening's rest,
looked hard into my eyes and with only
the slightest glimmer of mischief said
I was the most falling-in-loving-est
boy he had ever seen or heard of,

because, of course, when he asked me
what had happened, what was my excuse,
I hadn't told him all the details, but
I had told him the truth, that I had
fallen in love again, only this time
with a beautiful Irish girl, like his.

EBB TIDE

We live in primitive
times — it's 1978
and we're well into
the new dark ages
that began with
the failure of the
French & American
revolutions — back
in the early 1800s

"Duh" says some 8-year-old
as the new expression
of self-consciousness
over "incorrectness"
or lack of 8-year-old
1978 sophistication —
whatever that is, still
creating turmoil in
the psyche and war
games in the defense
of sensitivity and
"sexism" ("you cunt")
in the expression of
hurt pride and dis-
illusionment again . . .

Nature can still put
the lights out, stop
the traffic in our
eyes as well as our
alleys and no one, no
one can outdo fate at
creating the coincidence
of image and success
(the mice and rats
still alive and thriving

along with the flies
and roaches, the future
no longer that sterile
dream of people plagued
with disease and the
shit of ignorance fermenting)

I dont wanna be alone
I dont wanna leave my
home I dont wanna come
undone I just wanna be
the one

       dont not invite me
my time

FUTURAMA

This is the future
Where are the moving sidewalks
and monorails and family rockets
and paper clothes and throwaway
— "throwaway?" — kids on
motorized bikes and rotting
highways and empty bars and
videotapes and hand held
movie cameras and Van Morrison
still singing "too late to stop now"

come back go back
get back set back
wetback halfback
straight back hardback
way back bad back
right back just back
got back left back
wing back hog back
fat back drop back
shot back sat back
answer back hit back
jump back out back
bare back soft back
win back take back
bend back hurry back
lay back back back

1979

"My heart is where it belongs."

-Jack Kerouac *Visions of Gerard*

COMING UP FROM THE SEVENTIES

the cleanhead black guy
no bush, no sky piece, no
nothing but short hair and
glasses leans out the car
window, shotgun side, to
yell at the neighborhood
bag lady, *my* neighborhood
bag lady, "Shut up!" and
I don't like it, it's my
neighborhood, not his, and
she ain't doing shit to any
one except herself, a once
obviously attractive woman
who some people mistake for
a once obviously handsome
man which seems intentional
on her part, a very savvy
bag lady, now all greasy
haired and filthy, babbling
her obscenities at the side
walk and street, sometimes
at the air, though she always
seems to be aware of passers
by, at least me, when I pass
by and glance at her, to
catch her eye, I don't know
why I always do that with
strangers on the street,
Rain says that's why I'm
always getting so much grief
especially threats of violence
because I look people in the
eye too directly and for too
long and that seems somehow
like a challenge, as it did
back in the 50s when I was

a kid and I'd catch the eye
of some other male kid whose
neighborhood I was passing
through or who was passing
through mine and inevitably
my stomach would drop as I
suddenly realized I was in
a battle of balls to see
who looked away first knowing
that if I didn't it would
mean an even more obvious
challenge like the finger
or the Italian salute and
then it would be too late
to look away without looking
like a sissy or a punk, a
scared shitless faggot whose
intense eye contact didn't
have anything to do with
the real male stuff of kicking
each other's teeth in as a
sign of interest, so I'd
fight or talk bad or sometimes
bluff my way into their backing
down, but I'd promise myself
never to stare so long and
directly again except at the
girls who when they stared
back made life sexy and even
scarier, because if they got
tough there was no way to
not feel humiliated, so here
I am, more than twenty years
later, still checking every
one's head out through their
eyes and trying to decide
where I am in their world,
always sure I'm there because

I looked at them, let them
see me, like the bag lady
who I'm sure must know me by
now when I catch her eye
between her profane lists
and the assholes who yell at
her for reasons I can't under
stand anymore than I could
the assholes who'd decide
two humans looking at each
other for more than a second
must mean one of them gets
beat up or somehow humiliated,
somewhere between the 50s and
now it seemed it would turn
out differently, I remember
the absolute thrill of the
first hippie who flashed a
big grin and the peace sign
or fist my way when I caught
his eye and the defiantly long
hair we shared, unsuspecting
how the 50s had prepared me
for his show of friendliness,
not aware yet of how signifi
cant and satisfying it could
be to gather in massive crowds
and never have a massacre, not
even a fight, unless it came
from the law, which only Nutsy
McConnel took on in the 50s I
went through, that's how he
got his name, jumping a cop
to prove his manhood at 15,
one 50s spring like this
last one of the 70s, my bag
lady and me as much a symbol
of the way the last three,

four, however many decades
it has taken to create the
styles we share that signify
no one time more than any
other and yet let me know
she is probably my age and
her the same if she reads
me like she does the world
that she survives in in ways
I once tried by choice and
then by imposition of forces
I could not control and so
avoid, proud that there but
for the will to see it through
as "free" as I can learn to
be go all the me's I never
fail to see when I look into
the eyes, except maybe the
mean and nasty ones that
can't abide the sight of
anyone less ready or unwilling
to survive their way, yet
maybe even they too reflect
a me I hate to see intolerant
toward the things I've been
or might become, though I
hope never so dismally or
inhumanly as that guy in that
car letting me know it's not
the future anymore it's just
another door we all pass through

37

going through it again
this time turning 37
seems to be the instigator
one of the first of the
outside world's difficult
labels I learned the meaning
of early — *me* — that is
what the nuns used it for
and then the cops when
explaining to my father
why they were escorting
me home from somewhere
that should have been all
innocent fun and a little
harmless sex or whatever
passed for that at that
age which was around 10,
11, 12 by 13 no longer
harmless or innocent to
them though I continued
to believe I was nothing
more than my own romantic
hero no matter what label
the cops or nuns invented
to make their prejudices
sound official and convince
my father that authority
is always right — see
what I mean about going
through it again — I'm
obsessed now and then,
usually around birthdays,
with the imbalance of
it all as it's gone by
me or through me or me
through it — there's

still always the joy,
and usually for the same
old reasons, expectations
of true love and success
meaning recognition for
the lasting influence my
style has had on the world
that pretends not to have
to acknowledge it someday,
sure world, you came up
with all this shit from
the tv right? or from
some fucking union ward-
robe person on some back-
lot or in some city's
old clothes warehouse —
no way, they follow us,
and we are few and very
precious to ourselves
despite the ways we let
the others push their
egos around the block,
the city, the world —
ours don't have to be
pushed, in fact can't
be, we're too in love
with our own innocence
and romantic possibilities
to have portable egos —
except in the sense of
where we go they go — our
egos — another one of
the outside world's terms
I learned fairly young as
it too was applied to me
but not by cops or nuns,
more likely young Jewish
girls who were so much

more sophisticated than
we wanted to be because
it always seemed a burden
as in fact it still does,
though now it matters less
as so many things do each
time another year passes
through on its way to my
personal myth, another of
their terms for the accu-
mulated details of my
movement through the
time and space that's
mine forever no matter
how some outsider tries
to make money or fashion
or fun of what will only
be theirs for now if at
all — shit, lost track
of it as my 9-year-old
son calls up to ask if
he can go to some movie
with some friends and I
say sure after grilling
him on the details which
he'll remember so differ-
ently than I will because
it's his going to the
movies and only my "sure"
and whatever else we
share which is con-
siderable, it's his own
personal mythology he's
collecting and sorting
through and some of my
terms are the outside
world's to him and his
little dicoed-out loft-

kid friends who think
Billy Joel understands
them better than their
rocknroll parents, in
fact dont care that we
might have been there
at the start, that's
our problem, their art

AMAZING LUST

So now I'm thirty-seven
and sometimes I still feel
like a fucking teenager
only lately, I've felt like
a real big teenager, which
I never felt like when
I really was a teenager,
then I felt super thin,
wiry, fast, clean, and
on my way to the most
exciting life anyone has
ever imagined, and in my
own inimitable but some
times ordinary way I guess
I sort of did that, went
on to lead a totally and
somewhat originally crazy
life full of attempts at
all kinds of ways of taking
a chance at making it big
without doing what I at
least always thought most
folks had to do to make
it big in this society,
meaning stuff like lying
or at least faking a lot
of stuff and being nice
to people you can't stand
or pretending to believe
stuff you don't believe
when all I really believed
in was me, and my lust,
that made me feel I was
special because nobody
else seemed to have the
same amazing lust I had

because anyone who came
on as full of lust as I
felt seemed a little
sleazy or at least suspect
while the rest who may
have seemed more human
seemed less driven by
their sexual desires,
while mine seemed both
overwhelming and totally
above suspicion, I mean
not only good but worthy,
and it was only the warped
perspective of a ruthlessly
money driven society that
misled the ladies who may
have interpreted my crazy
hunger for their bodies
as something less than
heroic and romantic and
mortal like the works
of art I found so many
women to be and eventually
some of the men as well,
though the kind of lust
that sent me chasing big
eyed boys and kindly men
was of a different sort,
a long time later in my
life when what I wanted
was simply some respect
and appreciation for the
wiry, fast living but
honest and well meaning
teenager trapped inside
this rapidly aging body
no longer as wiry and
full of the future as it

may once have been and
the men often did that
or did something that
somehow served the same
purpose, made me feel
above suspicion for my
crazy desires, just a
man with lots of love
and lust to share with
anyone generous enough
to accept and maybe even
reciprocate, what a
waste it seems now to
have been so clumsy to
have been misunderstood
by anyone I ever ached
for and never knew that
way, despite the hundreds,
I guess thousands I did
in some way collaborate
with on whatever our lust
created for us, I have
to admit I don't remember
them all and sometimes
at a crowded party or
opening or any event
where people are into
looking good and the old
hunger is raging in me
still despite the fact
I may not intend to do
anything about it
invariably I run into
someone who seems to
know me intimately and
I wonder if we just
flirted sometime somewhere
we both were high and

loose or if in fact it's
one of the many I can
no longer remember,
despite my romantic
fantasies and pride in
never forgetting a face,
but faces look so different
when the body they belong
to is naked and expressing
its own crazy lust and
anyway my memory is
growing more and more
fragmented and full of
holes and I can't do much
about it except try
lecithin pills which
Charlie Walsh assured me
helped him learn Japanese
so fast and all I could
think of as he told me
this was not his crazy
compulsion to become a
servant of the government
and spend some years in
Japan but what crazy and
beautiful oriental bodies
he would now have the chance
to share his crazy Irish-
American one with as I am
lately convinced that, at
least here in the USA, it
is the orientals who have
the flash and potential
style to bring some new
energy and hope to the
arts and life in general
but especially sexiness
as we have experienced it

178

through movies, rocknroll,
and high and low fashion,
which often has nothing
to do with sexiness when
the clothes come off, I
mean I've been to bed with
some totally boring women
and men who looked un-
believably sexy in their
clothes and vice versa,
once I passed a man on
the street who looked so
conservative and bland
I wouldn't have noticed
him except he had these
almost crazed intense
dark eyes that locked
on mine for enough of
a second to startle me
into recognition that
this otherwise undis-
tinguished stranger had
once lovingly caressed
my cock with his mouth
in a steam room in one
of the two baths I have
ever gone to, the Club
Baths in New York on a
cold winter snowy night
in 73 or 74, I remember
how clean and bright and
hopeful like a kid's
Christmas eve the world
looked when we emerged
from the heat and steam
into the early morning
streets, and in my mind
the expression on the

face of this stranger I
later passed without
acknowledging except
for that split second
connection of the eyes
so different from that
night when afterwards
in the shower I saw him
watching me enjoying
washing myself off and
when I smiled he made
a gesture with his hand
to his mouth like I-
talian cooks do in tv
ads to indicate the
food is absolutely
delicious or divine,
such appreciation is
all I guess I want,
especially from those
I don't know because
somehow through them
you can really extend
the personal mythology
we all must create to
survive, because they
didn't really know us
while we were merely
alive, they knew us
when we were immortal

THE DEFINITE ARTICLE, THE INDEFINITE ARTICLE, AND THE GENUINE ARTICLE
for Terence Winch

I sat down among you
like a Bible salesman
encouraging prayers and
the study of the good book

only the good book was
mine and the prayer was
not only not divine worship
but profane expression of

a desire so full of lust
it must be the antidote
to all we were taught
that left us guilt ridden

but sharp willed and
wise around the issues
of survival and the void.
On the other hand, you

could control more than
could control you and
without losing any power
only sometimes you chose

to let it wither on
the way to happiness
because it didn't seem
to be the ultimate in

terms of what we always
suspected love could do
to satisfy our desire
through which we manifested

our own semi-divine natures
to everyone we could reach
cause after all we've both
been wired by the same

hot box, so to speak,
leaving us at least so-
phisticated if not suc-
cinct (words I always

thought should be avoided
as though inoculating us
against the diseases they
insisted expressed the most

intense forms of the
imaginative drives, etc.)
I mean, to share some
ex-lovers and ex-friends

as well as current friends
and mentors, fans, and
followers, modes and moods,
and even "articles of

clothing" and some foods
is pretty amazing for
such competitive and
ambitious and intensely

protective survivors
of the Catholic childhood
shepherding as well as
the academic anti-intuitive

benign neglect policy,
and on top of that we're
sporadically hot and
handsome and above the

petty prejudices that
include an anti-Irish bias
in the interpreting of
not only contemporary

political history but
contemporary literary
history as it's being
written and created in

our loveable USA. We are
not only the Coleridge and
Wordsworth of our times,
the Shelley and Keats, the

Eliot and Pound, the
Williams and Zukofsky,
the Ashbery and O'Hara,
the Jimmy Schuyler and

Edwin Denby, the Reznikoff
and Oppen, Bukowski and
d.a. levy, Bogart and Bacall,
the Doug Lang and Diane

Ward, we are the Lally and
Winch of future generations'
astoundment at our prolific
(critics call it "prolix")

series of perspectives on
the urban/suburban survival
hipness of our times and thus
the true heirs to the main

enduring art of what the others
call "*the* people" meaning all
of us who never intended anything
less than to demonstrate the art

of survival as the ultimate
expression of the kind of class
that goes without saying and
almost makes up for the past.

"AS TIME GOES BY"

I'm getting crazy again about time,
the voices of the kids outside chanting
something I can't quite make out like
Matty had a chocolate cake chocolate cake
to Mary had a little lamb and I can't stand
how it all goes on someday without me
so afraid suddenly of what that might mean
that we can never know, you know what I mean?
Like the sound of Nat King Cole's voice
soothing me earlier suddenly pisses me off
because it locates so accurately a memory
in me still living of an exact time in
my own life when romance was represented
by the teenaged affairs of my older sisters
and I worked overtime to trace the address
of a girl I had seen on the street one day
and finding it calling her up to say how
much I wanted to see her and her unable
to resist since we were both so young
it had to be the first time anyone ever
did that to her, or for her, or at her, and
now it's gone and what do you care it
wasn't your life and Nat King Cole singing
"somewhere along the way" means something
else to you or nothing, and that's what
most of my writing and life has been
about, the attempt to make my memories
yours so I don't have to be so scared
of it all meaning nothing when it has
to mean everything to make my heart
fill up like this and my head resonate
with the better than movies images of
the best and most enduring parts of
my life in the 40s and 50s and 60s and
it's like listening to Charles Ives is
so much easier because that don't mean

shit in my life specifically except
the accident of discovering how much
I like to listen to his piano works
that don't get in the way of my own
work by making me so conscious of my
past and the sweet fantasies of what
the future I have already passed through
would bring that it didn't or did at
times but so different and unexpected
and sometimes unaccepted because so
much more dependent on fucking time
outside my heart and memories instead
of in my head the way it started, like
this impulse to write about how fucking
crazy time can get to me though not
all the time, just some of the time,
like some of the light and some of
the sound and some of the ways we
still get around the inevitable . . .

THIS TIME

in back of us
of me there is
of me something
of me and some
cold thing some
push from some
cold space I
knew was there
but never anti
cipated of me
and my spaces
in which I grew
so restful on
the watch I'd
so carefully
learned of me
in back of all
experience as
I had known it
might be and was
without many
cold spaces
pushing anyone
and now it's
me

*

nobody can give you dignity

somebody must have said

though not to me

except me

*

I used to write like this too

I still do

*

I thought I had it

many times

every time

it had me

*

nobody knows

we even forget ourselves

just getting by

let alone

making it

*

only everybody knows
when you make it
thats why you
want to make it
only thats not how
or why you do
what you think you
have to do
because its what
you do to make it
188

for yourself
only
hardly anybody knows
about that
or how
or why
or even it
although
you love it
even when it
doesnt make it
goddamn

*

goddamn

it

*

or hot

or wet

or set

   or

*

get back
get there
get it
anything
better than
get by
just getting

by myself
aint getting
it
it's
not even there
like most of
history
in the air
around you
and that
clear or

unclear unclean

cold hot wet thick

tense heavy humid

opaque familiar

necessary old

*

this time

is just

another

time

*

love

and whatever induces it

and what passes for it

passes for it

*

I dont know

BIG DEAL

January is the cruelest month.
Sometimes I can't believe I
live like this, still. I'm
trembling as I write this, from
the fucking cold that charges
through the cracks and gaps of
this old loft and kicks the ass
of the outlaw gas heater. I
remember promising myself I'd
always live in apartments where
at least the janitor, or "super,"
lived, if not the landlord.
Usually small places were the
best and easiest to manage.
Just like I promised myself
once I'd never buy anything
on credit or too fancy with
extra features that meant more
things to go wrong. So here
I am, freezing in this stupid
loft, telling you about it on
an expensive, fairly new,
electric portable typewriter
that doesn't make the g's and
d's (I have to repeat them
several times to make a faint
impression so you'll never
really know what I mean), and
over ten thousand dollars in
debt to credit companies and
friends (I also made a resolu-
tion never to borrow money
from friends), so here it is
the dawning of another, more
promising decade, and me with
resolutions up the ass that
192

could have kept me from my
present frustrations and misery.
I have this terrible fore-
boding that the entire decade
will be spent extricating
myself from the results of
breaking the resolutions I
had made for the last one and
the one before that. Although
that's some kind of positive
note, that I've had the chance
to make and break so many
resolutions for more than a
few decades now. I think I
once resolved I'd never
make it this far too, unless
I was still young at heart,
in love with love, and ready
for some action when it
comes. And despite the
fucking freezing air in
here I do feel young, and
ready for whatever might
break, even if it means
my heart again. What is
it makes us keep believing
in our fucked up incon-
sistent selves. Our fucked
up inconsistent selves?
Like now I'm gonna trust
my memory to tell me what's
important in my mind and
heart that's gone down as
a year's unforgettable
emblem in my life, like
1970 and the massacres
at Kent and Jackson States,
or 1974 when Candy Darling

died, and 1972 I got back
into men in sexual ways
after a lapse of 19 years,
or 1971's Mayday DC fun,
we almost won, despite
the defeatist jive of
self-annointed leaders,
or 1975 when Patti Smith
seemed to come alive in
ways I'd thought only
some of us guys understood,
in 1973 I got back into
women after a lapse of
a year and Karen Allen's
eyes began that trend,
O 1979 you'll always be
the year I finally tried
my movie star fantasies
out and found they worked
so far, as opposed to
1977's trip of suit and
tie bit to find out if
I'd really missed some
kind of different ad-
venture in *those* jobs,
1978 saw me act on the
conclusion I had not,
did I forget 76's heart
break and denials, my
confusion over suddenly
discovering I had no
copyright on styles I
thought we'd made so
solidly our own what
seemed so never long
ago. Big deal, my memory
is always one I find
myself the center of,
194

though when it flashes
in the language of the
heart it tells me there
is no other self but
love. Except that was
the seventies when we
knew differently. We
thought. Didn't we?